Richard Ferdinand Wüerst, Maynard Butler

Elementary Theory of Music and the Treatment of Chords

Fifth Edition

Richard Ferdinand Wüerst, Maynard Butler

Elementary Theory of Music and the Treatment of Chords
Fifth Edition

ISBN/EAN: 9783337088088

Printed in Europe, USA, Canada, Australia, Japan

Cover: Foto ©Thomas Meinert / pixelio.de

More available books at **www.hansebooks.com**

ELEMENTARY THEORY

OF

MUSIC,

AND THE

TREATMENT OF CHORDS,

BY

RICHARD WÜERST.

*DIRECTOR AND PROFESSOR OF MUSIC AND MEMBER OF THE
ROYAL ACADEMY OF ARTS, BERLIN, PRUSSIA.*

———————

INTRODUCED FOR USE IN THE NEW ACADEMY OF TONE-ART AND THE CONSERVATORY OF MUSIC IN BERLIN.

———————

TRANSLATED INTO ENGLISH BY

MAYNARD BUTLER.

———

FIFTH EDITION.

———

PUBLISHED BY

THE BOSTON MUSIC CO.,

BOSTON, MASS.

To

Professor Theodore Kullak.

In dedicating this little work to you, my dear friend, I do so with the double pleasure of presenting you with a small token of my regard and admiration, and also as an expression of my appreciation of the fact that the experience which enables me to put this book before the public, has been gained, for the most part, in the course of the instruction given for so many years, in the Institution of which you are the Director. In this two-fold sense, I beg you to accept it from

Yours faithfully,

RICHARD WÜERST.

Berlin, June 1, 1867.

TO

Helen Vincent and Jeanie Welles Ringland

THIS

TRANSLATION IS DEDICATED

WITH THE

REMEMBRANCES

OF

Maynard Butler

BOSTON, MASS.

Introduction.

My object in compiling this work, has been to provide students of music with a book as brief, practical, and yet complete as possible, which should contain everything that each one of them ought to learn and could learn.

I have, therefore, extended its limits only as far as Modulation (which is a branch requiring study beyond the scope of the present undertaking) and have stopped at the point where the material for Chords and how to deal with them, under all circumstances, with figured bass, has been made clear; for my object has been to write a book suitable for *all* students, not for a favored few. There is in the work itself nothing new, but I do believe that the concise and, as it seems to me, clear manner in which its contents are presented, are my own, and but the natural result of the experience of fifteen years of teaching harmony. I should regard it as the most grateful result of my labor, if, by means of it, the preparatory studies of those who devote themselves to music should be made easier, their circle of knowledge enlarged and their interest in it increased; and that of these, they who possess talent, might acquire through it, a more thorough foundation of the theory of their art, than, alas! they too frequently possess.

RICHARD WÜERST.

CONTENTS.

ELEMENTARY THEORY.

A *Musical Tone* is a Sound of *fixed* height or depth : the collection of musical tones is called the *Musical System* : this System is designated by seven names ;

English — C, D, E, F, G, A, B.
German — C, D, E, F, G, A, H.
French — Ut, Re, Mi, Fa, Sol, La, Si.
Italian — Do, Re, Mi, Fa, Sol, La, Si.

These seven names naturally recur again and again, and upon the repetition of the first, which is then called the *Eighth*, the scope which they embrace is termed an OCTAVE.

The lowest octave which receives, in technical language, an especial name, is the *Contra Octave;* then follow the *Greater Octave*, the *Lesser Octave*, the First, Second, Third-lined, etc.*

The two divisions into which *Tone Color* in music is separated are *Major* and *Minor;* in German, *Dur* and *Moll.*

The Musical *Staff* consists of five *Lines*, the *lowest* of which is called the *first*: the notes outside the Staff are indicated by means of *added lines*, which are to be regarded simply as a continuation of the staff itself.

A *Musical Clef* is a sign which specifies a certain place upon the staff and affixes an unchangeable name to it; there are *three* such *clefs:*

The Violin or G Clef which is placed upon the second line, and gives to that line the name, *One-lined* G.

The *Bass* or *F* Clef which is placed upon the *fourth* line, and gives to that line, the name, *Lesser F.*

---

* In the absence of lines of the staff the tones of the Greater Octave are designated by large letters, and those of the Lesser by small ones; as C, the Greater Octave; c, the Lesser; c̄ the first-lined; etc.

The *C* Clef which gives to the line upon which it is placed the name, *One-lined* or *Middle* C.

This is divided into three kinds:

a. The Discant or Soprano Clef upon the *first* line ;

b. The *Alto* Clef upon the *third* line ;

c. The *Tenor* Clef upon the *fourth* line ;*

A table of these five Clefs would be thus represented:

---

* It was the custom, formerly, to divide the Violin Clef into *Violin* and *High Violin* Clefs, the latter being written upon the *first* line. The Bass Clef was written for *Baritone* upon the *third* C clef, for *Mezzo-Soprano,* upon the *second* line. The sign for the C clef was also made thus :—

Table of Notes in the Five Clefs.

VIOLIN.

SOPRANO OR DESCANT.

ALTO.

TENOR.

BASS.

Contra octave.	Greater Octave.	Lesser Octave.	One-lined Oct.	Two-lined Oct.	Three-lined Oct.	Four-lined Oct.

RHYTHM has a two-fold significance in music: it refers both to *duration* of time and to *stress:* the first, relates to *Notes* and their equivalent *Rests;* the second, to *Measure.*

NOTES* are divided into:

Whole

Half

Quarter

Eighths

Sixteenths

Thirty-seconds

Sixty-fourths

etc.

Notes to be written *above* the third line on the staff, are turned *down,* toward the *left;* those *below* the third line are turned *up,* toward the *right;* those *on* the third line may be turned down or up, according to convenience.

For Example:

In cases like that of the six sixteenths the majority of the notes govern the direction in which the stems of all are to be written— upward or downward.

RESTS are divided into the Whole Rest which *hangs* from a a line and fills one-half of a space.

---

* Formerly, other notes were in use than those adopted to-day. One of these — the Brevis, which has the value of eight quarter notes—is, in rare instances, still to be met.

The Half Rest ≖ which *lies* upon the line and fills one-half of a space.

Quarter Rest 𝄽 or less frequently 𝄼.

Eighth Rest ⌐.

Sixteenth Rest ⌐.

Thirty-Second Rest ⌐.

Sixty-Fourth Rest ⌐.

The *Double Whole* Rest ▭ which fills a whole space.

The *Four-Measure* Rest ▯ which fills two spaces.

If a number of measures is to be held, their equivalents; are to be combined out of the rests just indicated, as ▭ or two heavy diagonal lines are written across a *single* measure, above which the desired number of measures to be silent, is indicated by numerals, as ▰

The Dot lengthens the *note* or the *rest* after which it is placed, *half* of its value: $\unicode{x1D15F}. = \frac{3}{4}$

The Double Dot lengthens the first dot, one-half of *its* value:

$$\unicode{x1D15E}.. = \frac{7}{8} \qquad \unicode{x1D15F}.. = \frac{7}{16}^{*}$$

The Triplet arises from the division of a single *note* or *rest* into three parts; these three parts taking the value of the note or rest next in order *below* the given note or rest. For example:

A group of *six* notes of equal value, of which the *first* and the *fourth* are accented is called a *double* triplet; for example, ; if however the *first*, the *third* and the *fifth* are accented, the group is called a *sextolet*. For example:

---

* Every successive dot lengthens the preceding one half of its value; more than two dots, however, very rarely occur.

Time, in music, is *Equality* of *Accent*.

Strictly speaking there are but two kinds of Time; Two-part time and Three-part time, but for the sake of convenience these are divided into Simple two-part time and Compound two-part time, and Simple three-part time and Compound three-part time.

* Simple two-part time includes, $\binom{4}{4}$, ₵, $\frac{2}{2}$, $\frac{2}{4}$, $\frac{2}{8}$.

Compound two-part time includes, $\frac{6}{4}$, $\frac{6}{8}$, $\frac{12}{8}$.

Simple three-part time includes, $\frac{3}{2}$, $\frac{3}{4}$, $\frac{3}{8}$.

Compound three-part time includes, $\frac{9}{4}$, $\frac{9}{8}$.

Table of Kinds of Time.

Two–Part:	In beating time, in directing, *two* beats take the following motion: 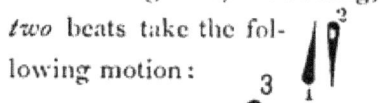
Simple: ₵, ₵, $\frac{2}{2}$, $\frac{2}{4}$, $\frac{2}{8}$.	
Compound: $\frac{6}{4}$, $\frac{6}{8}$.	
Three–Part:	*Three* beats:
Simple: $\frac{3}{2}$, $\frac{3}{4}$, $\frac{3}{8}$.	
Compound: $\frac{9}{4}$, $\frac{9}{8}$.	*Four* beats: 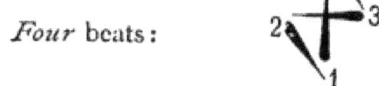

Compound $\frac{6}{8}$ time is derived, as the student should notice, from $\frac{2}{4}$ time by resolving every *quarter* note into a triplet of eighth notes: $\frac{6}{4}$ time, from $\frac{2}{2}$ time by resolving every *half* note into a triplet of *quarter* notes: $\frac{12}{8}$ time, from $\frac{4}{4}$ time by resolving every *quarter* note into a triplet of *eighth* notes.

Compound $\frac{9}{8}$ time is derived from $\frac{3}{4}$ time by resolving every *quarter* note into a triplet of *eighth* notes: $\frac{9}{4}$ time, from $\frac{3}{2}$ time by resolving every *half* note into a triplet of *quarter* notes.†

Although $\frac{5}{4}$ and $\frac{7}{4}$ time have been used in certain cases, they are so unsatisfactory to the innate feeling of rhythm, that they are not to be recommended for whole compositions.

---

* If the quarter-notes of four-four (𝄴) time are to be so played as to include two at every beat, this is called alla breve (from the Italian "in short manner ") time, and is marked ₵. This alla breve is the same as $\frac{2}{2}$ time.

† Of course, it follows that from $\frac{3}{8}$, $\frac{6}{16}$, and from $\frac{3}{8}$, $\frac{9}{16}$ can be evolved; but these divisions rarely appear.

An Incomplete Measure is an unfinished measure at the *beginning* of a composition, which upon repetition must be completed by its *closing* measure.

The Tie connects two notes lying upon the same interval, in such a manner as to make them sound but as one note.

The Syncope connects notes lying upon the same interval in such a manner as to make them accented against the natural rhythm.

The Fermate or Pause ⌢ indicates that the *note* or *rest* over which it is placed, is to have a longer duration than its natural value in the measure would indicate.

The Sign of Repetition ‖ or ‖ indicates that the measures preceding it, either from the beginning of the composition or from a sign like itself, are to be repeated.

Repetition may also be indicated by the words *da capo* — meaning "from the beginning" — contracted *D. C.*

If one part of the composition is to be repeated, the Signs § or ⸎ may be placed before it, and *da capo, d'al Segno,* (contracted, *D. C., D. S.*), meaning "from the Sign" written after it.

If the Repetition is to refer to several measures only, a large phrasing mark (slur) may enclose them and the word bis — "twice" — be written above it.

Every measure has its chief accent upon the first part of the measure; in measures divided into *two* parts, the first part has the *chief* and the second part the *secondary* accent; in those divided into three parts the first part has the *chief* and the two other parts the *secondary* accents.

In $\frac{4}{4}$ and $\frac{12}{8}$ time, the former being but a combination of two $\frac{2}{4}$ measures and the latter, of two $\frac{6}{8}$ measures, the *third* quarter in $\frac{4}{4}$ and the seventh eighth in $\frac{12}{8}$ time, receive an accent. In short, all those parts of a measure which are the initial note of a triplet, receive a slight accent.

The following table shows the various kinds of measure with their different accents.

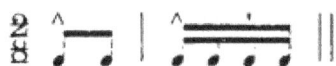

The following example shows into how many different forms rhythm can be separated.

The Degree of Motion in which a composition is to be executed is, amongst musicians, almost universally indicated by the Italian so-called Tempo Signs, the chief of which are : *

1. *For the Slowest Motion*, Largo, Adagio, Lento, Grave.

2. *For Moderately Slow Motion*, Larghetto, Andante, Andantino.

3. *For Moderately Fast Motion*, Allegretto, Moderato, Allegro moderato, Allegro ma non troppo.

4. *For Fast Motion*, Allegro, with various additional qualifying words, as:— Allegro con moto, Allegro con brio, Allegro con fuoco, Allegro animato, Allegro agitato, Allegro vivace, Allegro appassionato, Allegro molto, Allegro assai.

5. *For the Fastest Motion*, Vivace, Presto, Prestissimo.

These signs refer to the tempo of the whole composition, and are written at the beginning of it, *above* the staff, in *large* letters.

The following signs have reference to a certain part of a composition, and are written also *above* the staff, but in *small* letters.

They are :— *For Slow Tempo*, meno mosso, meno moto, meno allegro, più lento.

For Faster Tempo, più mosso, più moto, più Allegro, più vivo, più stretto.

The following signs refer to a few measures and are written *under* the staff in small letters. They are :

Ritenuto, ritardando, rallentando, calando ; indicating a slackening of the tempo.

Accelerando, stringendo ; a hastening of the tempo.

A tempo or tempo primo ; the return to the original tempo.

L'istesso tempo ; the same tempo.

Poco a poco ; little by little : as Stringendo poco a poco, means gradually growing faster.

---

* Some German composers — notably Schumann and his followers — have not made use of the usual Italian tempo signs, but of their German equivalents. The former language being universal amongst musicians is, of course, preferable in this particular.

Yet the student of music is recommended to make himself master of the German language, not only because by so doing he opens up to himself a world of interest in connection with his art, but because without a knowledge of it he cannot be thoroughly familiar with the literature of music. Indeed, those looking to the profession of music cannot take rank, amongst artists, without some knowledge of it.
— *Translator.*

Colla parte means that all the accompanying parts are to subordinate themselves to one part, which, for the moment, is to be made especially prominent.

DYNAMIC SIGNS, or those which determine the degree of the force of a tone, almost without exception, appear in the contracted form of the words, and are written *under* the notes with which the degree of force is to begin. The significance of these signs remains until a new sign appears. They are:

ff	fortissimo	=	very loud.
f	forte	=	loud.
mf	mezzo-forte	=	half loud.
p	piano	=	soft.
pp	pianissimo	=	very soft.
cresc.	crescendo	=	increasing in volume.
decresc.	decrescendo ⎫	=	decreasing in volume.
dim.	diminuendo ⎭		
	morendo	=	dying away.
	perdendosi	=	losing itself.
sf.	sforzato ⎫	=	refer only to the single notes under which they are placed, and indicate a stronger accent.
rinf.	rinforzando ⎭		

TONES in music are divided into *Whole* and *Half* tones.

Half tones are formed by tones upon neighboring degrees of the staff, between which no third tone can be placed.*

CHROMATIC SIGNS. The signs by means of which the half tones formed from the original seven natural tones of the musical scale, are indicated, are called Chromatic signs. They are:

♯	=	the sharp.
♭	=	the flat.
×	=	the double sharp.
♭♭	=	the double flat.
♮	=	the natural sign.

The ♯ raises the note before which it is placed, a half tone.

The ♭ lowers the note before which it is placed, a half tone.

The × raises the note before which it is placed, two half tones.

---

* Formerly theorists talked also of *large* and *small* half tones, or *major* and *minor* half tones. But this is a bit of pure pedantry, which adds nothing to the practical understanding of the subject.

The ♭♭ lowers the note before which it is placed, two half tones.

The ♮ renders the sharp, flat, etc., before a note, invalid, and restores it to its natural position before the chromatic sign was placed before it.

A × or ♭♭ demands a ♮♮ to remove it. If a note has had a × or ♭♭ before it and it is to have only one of those signs removed, one ♮ is placed before it and one of the signs required — *i.e.* a sharp or a flat.

For Example:

EXHARMONIC is the name of the series of notes by which the various ways of writing one and the same tone are indicated.

Enharmonic Table.

Enharmonic Tones.

Simple Tones.

Enharmonic Half Tones.

THE SCALE is a succession of tones ascending and descending at given distances.

Upon examination of these distances it will be found that *two whole* tones are followed by *one half* tone, then *three whole* tones and again a *half* tone.

$$1 \quad 1 \quad \tfrac{1}{2} \quad 1 \quad 1 \quad 1 \quad \tfrac{1}{2}$$

The above scale, in which the whole and half tones follow one another, after the formula $2\tfrac{1}{2}$ and $3\tfrac{1}{2}$, is called the Diatonic

Major Scale, and from its initial note C, C Major ———— or the Scale of C Major.

If the Diatonic Major Scales are to be formed upon every interval, of course, harmonic signs, flats, sharps, etc., must be brought into requisition in order to preserve the proper order of succession. Those *harmonic signs* which are in each individual case essential to the formation of the Diatonic Major Scale, are placed, however, not before each note, but at the beginning of the whole composition which is to be written in this *Key*, or form of tone coloring. These signs effect the whole composition, are placed at the beginning of it, and are called the *Signature*.

Other harmonic signs, appearing in the course of the composition extend their significance only over a single measure.

Table of Signatures of Major Keys.

C   Major without Signature.
G   "   with one sharp, f sharp.
D   "   with two sharps, f and c sharp.
A   "   with three sharps, f, c and g sharp.
E   "   with four sharps, f, c, g and d sharp.
B   "   with five sharps, f, c, g, d and a sharp.
F♯ "   with six sharps, f, c, g, d, a and e sharp.
C♯ "   with seven sharps, f, c, g, d, a, e and b sharp.

F   Major with one flat, b flat.
B♭ "   with two flats, b and e flat.
E♭ "   with three flats, b, e and a flat.
A♭ "   with four flats, b, e, a and d flat.
D♭ "   with five flats, b, e, a, d and g flat.
G♭ "   with six flats, b, e, a, d, g and c flat.
C♭ "   with seven flats, b, e, a, d, g, c and f flat.

Signatures are thus indicated:

There are two Minor scales: the Harmonic and Melodic.

Minor scales are derived from major scales by lowering certain intervals of the major scale of the same name. To form the Harmonic Minor Scale of C, for instance, the *third* and *sixth* intervals are lowered in C major. For example:

The Melodic Minor Scale of C, by lowering the third in ascending and the seventh, sixth and third in descending. For example:

The Signatures of minor scales are derived from those harmonic signs which appear in the *descending* melodic minor scale; as C minor with three flats, b♭, e♭, a♭.

The major and minor scales which have the same signatures are called Parallel (or relative) Scales.

The parallel minor scale to every major scale is found upon the third interval below the foundation tone or initial note of that scale. For example E♭ major has C minor for its parallel, both having the signature three flats.

The following Circle, called the Circle of Fifths, from the regular progression in fifths, of the successive scales, shows the proper arrangement of major and minor keys, with their signatures.

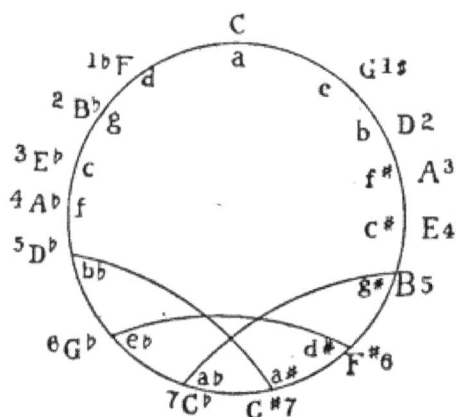

The major scales are on the outside of the circle; those with sharps to the right; those with flats to the left; on the inner side, are the minor scales, each opposite to its parallel major scale.

The marks in the lower part of the circle indicate the Enharmonic Scales.

The Chromatic Scale is a succession of half tones, and arises from the combinations of all those steps and half steps which do not appear in the Diatonic Scale.

In order to avoid a superfluity of enharmonic signs, the chromatic scale is so written that in ascending, the steps belonging to the original scale are *raised* and in descending they are lowered. For example:

It has become the custom amongst theorists to give fixed names to certain tones of each key, for the purpose of clearness in the study of harmony and of musical form.

The initial note or Foundation Tone of every key, is called *The Tonic;* the fifth tone *above* the foundation tone, *The Upper Dominant;* the fifth tone *below* the foundation tone, *The Lower Dominant,* or *Sub-Dominant;* the third tone *above* the foundation tone, *The Upper Mediant;* the third tone *below* the foundation tone, *The Lower Mediant;* the seventh tone of the scale is called *The Leading Note.*

The following formula shows the above terms as applied to C major.

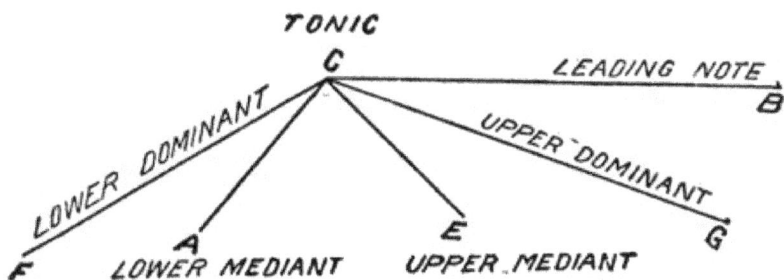

An Interval is the distance from one tone to another. Intervals are divided into Major, Minor, Augmented and Diminished.

A minor interval is a half tone smaller than a major; an augmented interval a half tone larger; a diminished interval two half tones smaller.*

In the Diatonic Major Scale all intervals formed with the tonic as their basis, are *major* intervals; if, therefore, any interval is to be measured, the lowest tone of it is to be considered as the tonic of a diatonic major scale, and if the upper tone of it lies in that scale, it is a *major* interval; if it is a half tone smaller, it is a *minor* interval; a half tone larger, an augmented interval; two half tones smaller, a diminished interval.

The Names of the Intervals are Primes or Unison, Seconds, Thirds, Fourths, Fifths, Sixths, Sevenths, Eighths or Octaves, Ninths and Tenths.

Hence, for example: the interval C — A would be a major sixth because the sixth tone in C major is A; C — A♭ a minor sixth; C — A♭♭ a diminished; C — A♯ an augmented sixth. If the lower tone of an interval to be classified, is f♭, g♯, d♯, a♯ or c♯ — upon which it is not customary (though it would be possible) to form diatonic major scales — the quickest way to decide their distances is to transpose the lower tone by means of enharmonic signs: as, for instance, if f♭ — a♭ is required, transpose f♭ into e and a♭ in g♯ and then regarding E as the tonic of the diatonic major scale E, from E — g♯ is a major third; in like manner b♯ — a, is transposed into c — b♭♭ and becomes a diminished seventh. The Examples under letter A at the end of the book are to be marked out by the pupil.

Chords.

A chord is the simultaneous sound of three or more tones placed in thirds, one above another.

The Major Triad consists of the foundation tone, its major third and its major fifth. In looking for the major triads in every key, one finds that they occur upon the 1st, 4th and 5th degrees of the scale in major keys, and upon the 5th and 6th degrees, in minor keys.

The Minor Triad consists of the foundation tone, its minor third and its major fifth. It is formed in major keys, upon the 2d, 3d and

---

* Many theorists call the major, prime, fifth, fourth and octave, perfect intervals; and the minor fifth, imperfect or, diminished; the names used above are certainly simpler and more consistent.

6th degrees of the scale; in minor keys, upon the 1st and 4th degrees.

The AUGMENTED TRIAD consists of the foundation tone, its major third and its augmented fifth. It is found only in minor keys and upon the third degree of the scale.

The DIMINISHED TRIAD consists of the foundation tone, minor third and minor fifth. It is found upon the 7th degree of the scale in major, and the 2d and 7th in minor keys.

The following shows the relative positions of all the triads in major and minor keys.

C major.

C minor.

Every interval of a triad can be doubled, *i. e.* it can appear at the same time in different octaves, or in different voices of the same octave. For example:

In writing chords with their four parts, the foundation tone of the triad is most frequently doubled; more rarely, the *third* or the *fifth*. If the 3d. lies in the uppermost part, (or voice) the position of the triad is called the position of the third; if the 5th, the position of the fifth; etc.

Position of the 3d. Pos. of the 5th. Pos. of the Octave. Pos. of the 3d. Pos. of the 5th. Pos. of the Octave.

THOROUGH BASS is simply the Stenography of Harmony.

In thorough-bass writing of chords, a bass note without any figure above or below it denotes that the triad of this note is meant. A *sharp, flat* or *natural* sign, above or below the bass note (without a figure) refers to the 3d. of the chord demanded. If any other interval is to be *raised*, the numeral designating it is placed above or below the bass note, and a mark drawn through it; if it is to be lowered, the necessary sign is placed before the numeral. For example:

The line at b denotes that the same harmony is to continue as far as the line extends.

The letters t. s. at c, stand for the Italian words, tasto solo, and denote that the bass is to have no harmony played with it. Other figuring of chords will be given as they appear in the course of the examples.

The chief rule in combining chords, is the following: Common tones should be kept in the same voice and octave; the other tones should move as little as possible.

In the above example, the bass note is doubled in every triad.

---

* When chords are to be written which demand notes outside the staff, they are denoted by means of added lines as in the chord of F major above. The same chord *below* the staff would be written thus:

Common tones are connected by curved lines (or ties).

Other examples of this kind will be found in the Appendix under B*. If there are no common tones, lead the voices in opposite directions; *i. e.*, the three upper voices in the opposite direction from the bass.

In the above example, common tones are bound together, and where there are none alike, straight lines show the opposite directions in which the parts move.

Further examples are to be found under C.

The next rule arises from the necessity of avoiding false progressions. False Progressions are the simultaneous movement of two or more voices in octaves, fifths or fourths.

At the example marked a, the bass and the fifth in both chords, move in the same direction; also the bass and its octave.

At example b, there are successive fourths; at c, the outer voices

---

* The student is advised to write each exercise in the three different ways, indicated above, following the same principle as to the doubling of the bass-note and the leading of the voices. Constant practice in playing the harmony to each of the basses given, without writing them out upon paper, is of the greatest importance.

b b♭, made what is called, in harmony, Cross Position. This occurs when neighboring tones upon the same degree of the staff appear in two successive chords, in different parts or voices. If, however, one part has both tones, (as in example d) the cross position no longer exists, as in the above example, where the upper voice has b as well as b♭ and the bass has b♭.

Progressions like the following example make the *impression* of being consecutive Octaves, Fifths and Cross Position, without, in the strictest sense of the word, being false. They are, therefore, called *Concealed* Octaves, Fifths, etc., and are to be as carefully avoided as direct octaves, fifths, etc.*

Exceptions† to the rule against the use of successive Fifths, Fourths, etc.

1. The minor 5th may follow the major 5th.

2. The augmented 4th may follow the major 4th.

3. Fourths, above or below which, another voice proceeds in successive thirds, *may* follow one another.

---

* Progressions of Seconds, Sevenths and Ninths are, of course, to be as carefully avoided as those just mentioned; but they are so extremely disagreeable to the ear, as may be readily proved by trying them upon the piano, that there is little danger of their appearing, and there are, therefore, no especial rules against their use.

† As the rule against the use of consecutive octaves, etc., is solely for the sake of beauty of sound, it is not to be observed when successive 5ths, 4ths, or even Cross Position sound well; as for instance in the following succession of chords.

Doubled Octaves, as they constantly appear, especially in orchestral compositions, are not to be confounded with consecutive Octaves.

At a there is a *Doubling* of the bass.

At b there is a *Doubling* of the upper voice.

At c there is a *Doubling* of the middle voice; but in all these cases there is no *false progression*.

Inversion.

If the several tones of a chord are so placed that another than the foundation tone lies in the bass, this is called *inverting the chord*.

The First Inversion of the Triad is that in which the third of the Triad lies in the bass. It consists of bass-tone, third and sixth, is called the chord of the 6th and is figured 6.

In four-part harmony the 6th interval of the chord of the 6th is most frequently doubled, more rarely the 3d, most rarely the bass-note.

The above example shows the chord of the 6th, first, at a, with doubled sixth; secondly, at b, with doubled third; thirdly, at c, with doubled bass tone.

It is advisable in the first exercises to be worked out by the pupil, to make use of that doubling of the sixth which produces the most agreeable effect upon the ear.

For example:

As *Contrary Motion* is *always* to be sought, it is well to make use of it even at times when the successive chords contain *common tones:* as for instance in the chords of the 6th upon c♯, b, a and g, in the above example.

As the bass in these instances always proceeds by one degree *upward*, the sixth in the lower voice should be kept stationary, and the three other voices proceed *downward* — not, as in the following example, which would not be so good because such a succession as is indicated by the marks, would produce the effect of *concealed octaves.*

For the same reason the d, in the chord of the 6th upon f♯ is held, in both voices as at N. B. instead of carrying it on to g, so that a *triad* with doubled fifth is produced. Further examples are to be found in the Appendix D.

If several chords of the 6th.follow one another, false progressions are avoided by doubling the sixth and the bass-note alternately; or by leading the chord of the sixth in contrary motion and doubling the bass-note several times. By sometimes doubling the third the disposition of the chords can also be improved.

For example:

In this example, six successive fourths appear in the first and the second staffs, but the bass notes to which they belong go in thirds to *one* of the voices of the chord, and thus the false progression is done away with. The other remaining voice of the three, changes with the doubling of the sixth and the bass-note, in order to avoid consecutive Octaves and Fifths. In the third staff, *contrary motion* prevails; in the second and third chords of the 6th, the *bass note* is to be found; in the fourth chord, the *third* appears; in the fifth the *bass-note* again and in the sixth chord, the *sixth* is doubled.

The chord of the 6th of the Diminished Triad, on the other hand, is especially agreeable with the doubled *bass-note*, but it frequently also appears with doubled *third* and with doubled *sixth*.

For example:

At c, there are consecutive Fourths in the middle voices, which by the descending of the F (in the upper voice) to E, produces an

---

* A succession of chords of the 6th may also be figured thus :

agreeable effect; at D, the upper b ascends toward C, and the
lower b descends towards G, because, otherwise, the outer voices
would produce the effect of Concealed Fifths. The handling of
the chords at e is also frequently to be met. Further examples in
Appendix E.

It is also most beneficial for the student to practice writing figured basses in the broad (or open) position of the chords; *i. e.*,
beyond the scope of an octave — making use of the three C clefs;
as, for example, in the following:

Further examples in Appendix F.

The Second Inversion of the Triad is the $\frac{6}{4}$ chord, in which the
Fifth of the Triad lies in the bass. It consists of *bass-tone*, *fourth*
and *sixth*, is figured $\frac{6}{4}$ or $\frac{4}{6}$ and appears in four-part harmony, almost always with *doubled bass-tone*. The chief exception to this
rule is in the $\frac{6}{4}$ chord of the Augmented Triad, when the bass-tone
should *not* be doubled as otherwise, consecutive octaves are
almost unavoidable, as, for example at N.B. in the following
exercise:

When a triad is to be played upon a bass-note which has just before appeared in figured form, the second of the two is to be marked with the numbers $\frac{5}{3}$, as is shown in the preceding example several times.

The $\frac{5}{4}$ chord or chord of the Fifth and Fourth is not to be regarded as an independent chord at all, but as a preparation for a major or minor triad, or a chord of the Dominant Seventh upon the same degree of the Staff. It consists of *foundation* tone, *major fifth* and *major fourth*. The foundation tone is almost without exception the tone to double.*

Further examples of the $\frac{4}{6}$ and the $\frac{5}{4}$ chords in the Appendix G.

---

* The inversions of the $\frac{5}{4}$ chord are even more than the original chord, of a *preparatory* nature. They sound like suspended 6 or $\frac{6}{4}$ chords, have no especial name, and are figured $\frac{2}{3}$ or $\frac{4}{7}$, as the case may be.

THE CHORD OF THE DOMINANT SEVENTH.

If to the Triad of the Upper Dominant a third (the third pecul-
iar to the natural progression of the scale, of which it, in each case,
forms a part) be added, the chord thus produced is called the
chord of the Dominant Seventh, which consists of *foundation tone*,
major third, major fifth and minor seventh, and is figured 7. This
exceedingly important chord necessitates the following of another
chord upon it, and this enforced succession is called its Resolution.

The proper resolution of the chord of the Dominant Seventh is
as follows: the *foundation tone* proceeds a *fourth upward* or a
fifth downward, but may also remain stationary. The *third* goes
one degree *upward*, the *fifth* and the *seventh* one degree *downward*; the *fifth*, however, may upon occasion, proceed *upward*.
From this resolution, in which the fifth proceeds downward, an incomplete triad is produced, with twice-doubled foundation tone and
third, as in a and b; if the foundation tone *remains* stationary, a $\frac{6}{4}$
chord is produced with doubled fourth, as in c.

When the fifth goes *upward*, as at d, an incomplete triad with
doubled foundation tone and doubled third is the result. At e, the
fifth proceeding *upward*, a $\frac{6}{4}$ chord with doubled sixth is the result.
As the chord of the *Dominant Seventh* is the same in major and
minor (the *harmonic* minor scale is, of course, meant), it can be
resolved into minor as well as major, as, for example, at e.

Further examples in Appendix H.

The Inversions of the Dominant Seventh chord are resolved after the same rule as the original chord, except the *foundation* tone, which in the inversions, *always* remains stationary.

The *First Inversion* is the chord of the Fifth and Sixth, which consists of *bass-tone, minor third, minor fifth,* and *minor sixth,* and is figured $\frac{5}{6}$ or $\frac{6}{5}$.

Example as follows:

Further examples in Appendix I.

The Second Inversion of the chord of the Dominant Seventh, is the Chord of the Third and Fourth, consisting of bass tone, minor third, major fourth and major sixth and is figured $\frac{3}{4}$ or $\frac{4}{3}$.

In the preceding example, the bass tone of the three-four chord is generally carried downward. As it, however, is the *fifth* of the original chord, it can, like it, move one degree upward. In the chord of the sixth thus produced, the doubling of the bass note should be avoided by taking the *third* of the $\frac{3}{4}$ chord a *fourth* downward; but this is not to be done when it lies in the upper voice.

Further examples in Appendix K.

The THIRD INVERSION is the chord of the Second, which consists of bass-tone, major second, augmented fourth and major sixth, and is figured 2. The resolution of the chord of the second, results without exception in a chord of the sixth, upon the degree or half degree *below* it.

Further examples in Appendix L.

Besides the regular resolution of the chord of the Dominant Seventh there are others, which, however, relate only to the *original* chord and not to the *inversions*. For instance:

1. The *third* may proceed a third downward.

2. The *three* upper voices may proceed one degree upward, if the *seventh* lies in a middle voice.

3. The fifth may be left out and the bass-note doubled instead of it, which then remains stationary in the resolution.

This last manner of treating the chord of the Dominant Seventh is the most agreeable to the ear, and the most convenient for the handling of the other parts of the chord. All of these *exceptional resolutions* of the chord of the Dominant Seventh have the advantage of producing a *complete* triad, that is, one in which all the intervals appear.

FIRST.

SECOND.

N.B.

THIRD
EXCEPTIONAL
RESOLUTION
OF THE CHORD
OF THE DOMI-
NANT SEVENTH.

At N. B. if the three upper voices were taken upward, consecutive fifths would appear; therefore, in this case (where the seventh does not lie in the middle voice) the *regular* resolution (as used above) or the first exceptional one is preferable. It is advisable for the pupil to write the exercises upon the chord of the Dominant Seventh, first with the regular and then with the three irregular resolutions.

Examples for this purpose are to be found in Appendix M.

If a third (that third which pertains to the scale to which the chord itself belongs) be added to the Chord of the *Dominant Seventh*, a chord is formed which is called the *Chord* of the *Ninth*:— in major, the *Major Chord of the Ninth*, in minor, the Minor Chord of the Ninth: it consists of foundation tone, major 3d, major 5th, minor 7th, and major or minor 9th and is figured 9.

The resolution of the chord of the ninth is the same as that of the chord of the Dominant Seventh, but the ninth always moves one degree downward; the fifth, however, which in the Dominant Seventh may move upward or downward, in the Chord of the Ninth *must* move *upward*, when it lies *under* the *ninth*, as it otherwise would make a false progression of *fifths* with it. In four-part harmony, however, the fifth is omitted altogether.

The student should note the fact, that the resolution of the *major* chord of the 9th is only in major, while that of the *minor* chord of the 9th is in both minor and major. In order to become familiar with the treatment of the fifth, the student is advised to write the chord of the 9th in both four and five part harmony, as in the following example:

Further examples in Appendix N.

The Inversions of the chord of the 9th are resolved after the same manner as the original chord; because of the accumulation of very closely neighboring tones, however, some positions are not allowable; while others, on the contrary, are not only allowable, but agreeable.

The FIRST INVERSION is the chord of the Sixth and Seventh, which consists of bass-tone, fifth, sixth and seventh and is figured $\frac{6}{7}$ or $\frac{7}{6}$. The most agreeable position of this chord is the following; the 6th next to the *bass-tone* and the 5th and 7th in the octave above it.

Bad.   Good.   Less agreeable, but frequently used.

The progression of the *foundation* tone of the original chord at e, though possible, is rare.

The SECOND INVERSION, is the chord of the Third and Second, which consists of bass-tone, second, third and fourth, and is figured $\frac{2}{3}$ or $\frac{3}{2}$.

The most agreeable position is the following: bass-tone, second, fourth and, above them, the third. The resolution of the $\frac{2}{3}$ chord is upon the chord of the 6th of the next degree below it or the half degree above it.

Bad.   Good.   Less agreeable, but frequently used.

The THIRD INVERSION is the chord of the second, the sixth and the seventh, which consists of bass-tone, second, sixth and seventh, and is figured $\frac{2}{6}{7}$ or $\frac{7}{6}{2}$.

The most agreeable position is that in which the intervals follow one another in the order of the figuring of the bass. The resolution is into the $\frac{6}{4}$ chord upon the degree *below* it.

The following is an example of the inversions of the chord of the 9th :

Further examples in Appendix, under O.

The Inversion of the chord of the ninth, in which the *fifth* lies in the bass, is only agreeable, when the five parts are represented ; as in the following example :

If the foundation tone of the major and the minor chords of the 9th be left out, a chord is formed which is called, in the one case, the Minor Chord of the Seventh ; and in the other, the Diminished Chord of the Seventh.

The Minor Chord of the 7th consists of foundation tone, *minor* third, *minor* fifth and *minor* seventh.

The Diminished Chord of the 7th consists of *minor* third, *minor* fifth and *diminished* seventh.

Both chords are figured 7, and are treated as parts of the chord of the 9th. The rule with regard to the fifth in the chord of the 9th, when it lies under the 9th, is, in the altered enumeration of the intervals, in the case of these chords of the 7th — as follows: the *third* of the minor and the Diminished chords of the 7th, *must* move *upward*, when it lies *under* the 7th.

Major Ch'd of the 9th. | Minor Ch'd of the 7th. | Minor Ch'd of the 9th.

Ch'd of the Diminished 7th.

The Chord of the Diminished 7th like the minor chord of the 9th, from which it is derived, can be resolved into both major and minor. Both chords — the minor and the diminished chords of the 7th — have three inversions, the $\frac{5}{6}$, the $\frac{3}{4}$ and the 2 chord, the tones of which move in the same direction as each does in the original chord.

In b, as the third of the original chord b, d, f, a, lies in the bass, the *seventh* must always lie above it, and the *bass-note* be led upward.

In the two chords of the 2d there is at d, first a regular and then an exceptional treatment of the chord, in which d moves upward, although it lies *above* a ; this is caused by the fact, that there would otherwise be a false progression of *fourths* with no *third* voice proceeding in *thirds* alongside it.

It is customary to use the rule exemplified at e rather than that at d, because it produces a more agreeable $\frac{6}{4}$ chord.

If uncertainty arises as to the best method of treating these chords of the 7th (which, it must always be remembered, are *derived* from the chord of the 9th), it is well to place the intervals composing them, one above another in thirds, and then add a major third, *below* the bass-tone, when, the chord of the 9th, from which it is derived, thus being formed, the treatment of the intervals will be clear.

Further examples in Appendix P.

The following table furnishes a view of all the chords thus far mentioned, with their derivations:

Table of Chords.

The Triad.

IN MAJOR KEYS.	IN MINOR KEYS.
Major triad upon the intervals 1, 4, 5 .	Upon 5, 6. Upon 1, 4.
Minor triad upon 2, 3, 6.	Upon 2, 7.
Diminished triad upon 7.	Augmented triad upon 3.

Inversions are the 6 and the $\frac{6}{4}$ chords.
The $\frac{5}{4}$ chord.

The Chord of the Dominant Seventh.
Figured 7.

Inversions are $\frac{5}{6}$, $\frac{3}{4}$ and 2 chords.

Major Chord of the 9th.	Minor Chord of the 9th.
Figured 9.	Figured 9.

Inversions are $\frac{6}{7}$, $\frac{3}{2}$ and $\frac{\overset{2}{6}}{7}$ chords.

Minor Chord of the Seventh.	Dim. Chord of the Seventh.
Figured 7.	Figured 7.

Besides these, there are *five* chords of the Seventh, which are derived by altering the intervals of the Dominant Seventh and the Diminished Seventh. These are called *Mixed Chords.*

The First Mixed Chord is derived from the Dominant Seventh chord by the lowering of its *third*, so that, for example, from g, b, d, f, the mixed chord g, b♭, d, f is produced. The treatment of it is explained in the following example:

The Inversions of the Mixed chords of the Seventh have the same names as those of the other chords of the Seventh. They are to be dealt with as are the original chords; in c, for example, the manner of resolving the $\frac{5}{6}$ chord is based upon that at a, in its original form. The *foundation* tone in the resolution of the inversions of the mixed chords, remains stationary, as it does in those of the Dominant Seventh.

The Second Mixed Chord is also derived from the Dominant 7th by the *lowering* of the *fifth*; from g, b, d, f; g, b, d♭, f is produced. This chord most frequently appears in its second inversion as $\frac{3}{4}$ chord.

The THIRD MIXED CHORD is formed by raising the *fifth* of the Dominant 7th chord. This raised fifth sounds best when it lies in the upper voice and ought to move a *half* tone *upward*.

At f and g two exceptions are introduced in which the bass-note lies *above* the raised fifth.

The FOURTH MIXED CHORD is formed by raising the seventh of the Dominant 7th chord. From g, b, d, f, the chord g, b, d, f♯ arises.

Example of Fourth Mixed Chord:

The FIFTH MIXED CHORD is derived from the *Diminished* Chord of the Seventh by lowering its *third*. From g♯, b, d, f, the chord g♯, b♭, d, f arises.

The consecutive *fifths* at c, are agreeable to the ear, and, hence, are frequently used; they are to be avoided only in the *outer voices*. It is advisable for the student to practice writing the eight chords of the Seventh by designating each by its name or the name of the chord from which it is derived, as in the following example:

D denotes dominant; M, minor; Dim., diminished; and each of the mixed chords is marked I, II, III, etc. with Roman numerals.

Table of the Intervals of the Eight Chords of the Seventh,

	Third.	Fifth.	Seventh.
Dominant Seventh Chord.	major.	major.	minor.
Minor Seventh Chord.	minor.	minor.	minor.
Dim. Seventh Chord.	minor.	minor.	diminished.
1st. Mixed Seventh Chord.	minor.	major.	minor.
2d. Mixed Seventh Chord.	major.	minor.	minor.
3d. Mixed Seventh Chord.	major.	augmented.	minor.
4th. Mixed Seventh Chord.	major.	major.	major.
5th. Mixed Seventh Chord.	diminished.	minor.	diminished.

Further examples in Appendix Q.

If the Dominant Seventh be resolved into other tones than those of the tonic, so-called *deceptive cadences* are formed, which, however, are employed only when the Dominant 7th chord appears *without doubled* bass-note.

The most important deceptive cadences are:

The last succession of Dominant 7th chords is best treated in the above manner; *i. e.*, by writing it alternately with all its tones, and then with the fifth omitted and the bass-tone doubled in its place. Common tones are thus employed, and the chromatic changes are kept in the same voices.

Deceptive cadences may be used in connection with the Inversions, as well as with the original chords. For example:

Further examples in Appendix R.

The chord of the diminished 7th offers the greatest possibility of modulation of all chords: from it, it is possible to go directly from one key into another and in the following manner:

1. Every inversion of the diminished 7th sounds like another diminished 7th chord, and, by means of enharmonic changes can be written as if it were and resolved accordingly. For example:

2. The same four modulations may be produced by keeping three tones stationary and moving a half tone downward with one. For example:

3. Or one tone may remain stationary and three move a half tone *upward*, and four new keys be reached.

4. If *three* tones move a whole tone and *one* a half tone *upward*, four new keys may be reached.

5. If *three* tones move a *half tone*, and *one*, a *whole tone*, *downward*, four new keys may also be reached.

6. The chord of the diminished 7th can be resolved into a $\frac{6}{4}$ chord upon the degree a *half* tone *higher*, or a *whole* tone *lower*.

7. All the tones of the diminished chord of the 7th can move, simultaneously, a *half tone upward* or *downward*. For example:

Further examples of the treatment of the diminished 7th chord in Appendix S.

APPENDICES.

Appendix A.

Name each of these intervals, making the major with m, the minor with min., the diminished with dim., the augmented with aug., and the distance of each interval by the corresponding numerals.

No. 1.

No. 2.

Find the tones which, with the tones given, will form the intervals indicated.

No. 3.

Aug. 5.   min. 7.   m. 7.   dim. 7.   min. 10.   m. 3.   min. 5.

m. 7.   m. 3.   aug. 5.   dim. 3.   aug. 2.   min. 6.   m. 3.

Appendix B.

No. 4.

No. 5.

No. 6.

Appendix C.

No. 7.

No. 8.

No. 9.

Appendix D.

No. 10.

No. 11.

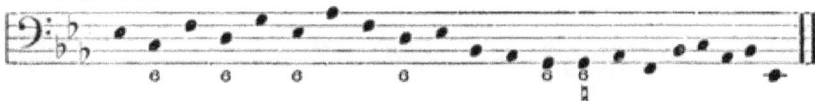

No. 12.

Appendix E.

No. 13.

No. 14.

No. 15.

Appendix F.

No. 16. *

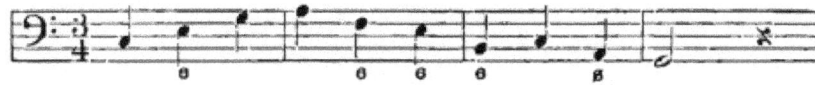

* The exercises divided into measures are to be written in score; i. e., in all the clefs.

No. 17.

Appendix G.

No. 18.

No. 19.

No. 20.

No. 21.

Appendix H.

No. 22.

No. 23.

No. 24.

Appendix I.

No. 25.

No. 26.

No. 27.

Appendix K.

No. 28.

No. 29.

No. 30.

Appendix L.

No. 31.

No. 32.

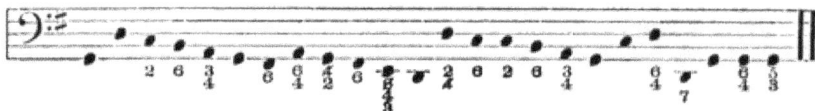

No. 33.

Appendix M.

No. 34.

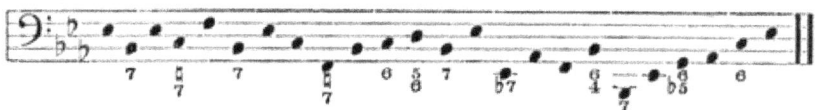

No. 35.

No. 36.

Appendix N.

No. 37.

No. 38.

Appendix O.

No. 39.

No. 40.

No. 41.

Appendix P.

No. 42.

No. 43.

Appendix Q.

No. 44.

No. 45.

No. 46.

Appendix R.

No. 47.

No. 48.

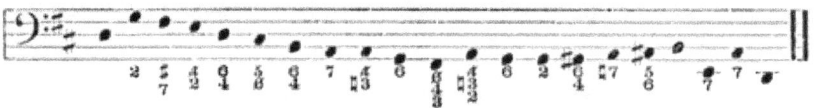

No. 49.

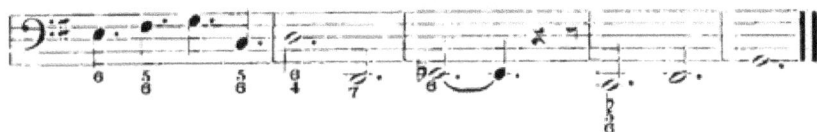

Appendix S.

No. 50.

No. 51.

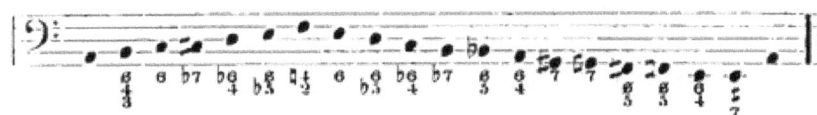

No. 52.